E
PLO

Plourde, Lynn.

Pigs in the mud in
the middle of the
rud.

$15.95

000029272
12/04/1997

	DATE		
Ca+2B2 2C2 C		9-30-1999	
	WITHDRAWN		

PIGS in the MUD
in the Middle of the Rud

BY **Lynn Plourde**

ILLUSTRATED BY

John Schoenherr

THE BLUE SKY PRESS
An Imprint of Scholastic Inc. · New York

THE BLUE SKY PRESS

Text copyright © 1997 by Lynn Plourde
Illustrations copyright © 1997 by John Schoenherr

Permissions Department, The Blue Sky Press, an imprint of Scholastic Inc.,
555 Broadway, New York, New York 10012.
The Blue Sky Press is a registered trademark of Scholastic Inc.
Library of Congress Cataloging-in-Publication Data
Plourde, Lynn.   Pigs in the mud in the middle of the rud [by Lynn Plourde;
illustrated by John Schoenherr.   p.   cm.
Summary: A feisty grandmother and her family struggle to get an assortment
of farm animals out of the road so the family can pass in their Model T Ford.
ISBN 0-590-56863-9
[1. Automobile driving—Fiction.   2. Domestic animals—Fiction.
3. Grandmothers—Fiction.   4. Stories in rhyme.]   I. Schoenherr, John, ill.
II. Title. PZ8.3.P5586922Pi 1997 [E]—dc20 96-23098 CIP   AC
12 11 10 9 8 7 6 5 4 3 2   7 8   9[9 0[0
Printed in the United States of America   36
First printing, March 1997

For Paul
with love and thanks
for never once saying,
"Won't do!"
—L. P.

For Claire
for not stopping
the silliness
—J. S.

It had rained. It had poured.
Now a Model T Ford
was stopped in the rud
by some pigs in the mud.

"Pigs in the rud!"
Grandma said.

Oh no. Won't do.
Gotta shoo. But who?

"I'll shoo. That's who,"
Brother said.

And he shooed.
And he squealed.
And he rutted.
And he reeled.

But the pigs didn't budge.
Not a tiny little smudge.

And she shooed.
And she clucked.
And she squawked.
And she plucked.

But the hens didn't scatter.
Not a tiny little smatter.

Oh no. Won't do.
Gotta shoo. But who?

"I'll shoo. That's who,"
Sister said.

"Hens in the rud!"
Grandma said.

"Sheep in the rud!"
Grandma said.

Oh no. Won't do.
Gotta shoo. But who?

"I'll shoo. That's who,"
Mama said.

And she shooed.
And she jeered.
And she baa-ed.
And she sheared.

But the sheep didn't shuffle.
Not a tiny little shmuffle.

"Bulls in the rud!"
Grandma said.

Oh no. Won't do.
Gotta shoo. But who?

"I'll shoo. That's who,"
Papa said.

10

And he shooed. And he tussled.
And he snorted. And he rustled.

But the bulls didn't charge.
Not a tiny little smarge.

Pigs, hens, sheep, bulls—all in the rud.
Brother, Sister, Mama, Papa—all in the rud.

Oh no. Won't do.
Gotta shoo. But who?

"OOOOOO-EEE! Up to me,"
Grandma said.

With her hands on her hips,
and a snarl on her lips,

and her dander up,
Grandma yelled, . . .

Budge, scatter,
shuffle, charge.
Smudge, smatter,
shmuffle, smarge.

All to sup.

At last, empty rud.

But look in the mud.

With her dress all rumpled,
and her bonnet all crumpled,
and muddy, head to toe. . .

Grandma said,
"Time to go!"